BUILDING VIRTUAL WORLDS

By
Kirsty Holmes

CRABTREE
PUBLISHING COMPANY
WWW.CRABTREEBOOKS.COM

CRABTREE
PUBLISHING COMPANY
WWW.CRABTREEBOOKS.COM

**Published
in Canada
Crabtree Publishing**
616 Welland Avenue
St. Catharines, ON
L2M 5V6

**Published in
the United States
Crabtree Publishing**
PMB 59051
350 Fifth Ave, 59th Floor
New York, NY 10118

Published in 2019 by Crabtree Publishing Company

Author: Kirsty Holmes

Editors: Holly Duhig, Petrice Custance

Design: Gareth Liddington

Proofreader: Melissa Boyce

**Production coordinator and
    prepress technician**: Margaret Amy Salter

Print coordinator: Katherine Berti

Photo credits:
All images are courtesy of Shutterstock.com.

Cover – , 2 – Swill Klitch, 4 – Swill Klitch, 5 – Giuseppe_R, Saikorn, Niphon Subsri, 10 – Blan–k, A–spring, Prostock–studio, adamziaja.com, 11 – GooGag, IconBunny, 12 - Tinxi, dennizn, 13 - dean bertoncelj, 18 – VitalityVill, 22 – pluie_r, 23 – Evan–Amos, Boffy b, Images are courtesy of Shutterstock.com. With thanks to Getty Images, Thinkstock Photo and iStockphoto.

Planet Coaster © 2018 Frontier Developments plc. All rights reserved.

Stardew Valley – ConcernedApe ©

Aven Colony: all images courtesy of Mothership Entertainment and Team 17. All rights reserved. With grateful thanks.

LEGO Worlds: all images courtesy of Warner Brothers Games. All rights reserved, With grateful thanks.

Printed in the U.S.A./012019/CG20181123

Library and Archives Canada Cataloguing in Publication

Holmes, Kirsty, author
        Building virtual worlds / Kirsty Holmes.

(Game on!)
Includes index.
Issued in print and electronic formats.
ISBN 978-0-7787-5257-8 (hardcover).--
ISBN 978-0-7787-5270-7 (softcover).--
ISBN 978-1-4271-2186-8 (HTML)

        1. Virtual reality--Juvenile literature. 2. Shared virtual environments--Juvenile literature. 3. Computer simulation--Juvenile literature. 4. Electronic games--Design--Juvenile literature. I. Title.

QA76.9.C65H65 2019   j006.8   C2018-906123-5
                                                         C2018-906124-3

Library of Congress Cataloging-in-Publication Data

Names: Holmes, Kirsty, author.
Title: Building virtual worlds / Kirsty Holmes.
Description: New York, New York : Crabtree Publishing Company, 2019. | Series: Game on! | Includes index.
Identifiers: LCCN 2018053423 (print) | LCCN 2018055651 (ebook) | ISBN 9781427121868 (Electronic) | ISBN 9780778752578 (hardcover : alk. paper) | ISBN 9780778752707 (pbk. : alk. paper)
Subjects: LCSH: Video games--Juvenile literature. | Virtual reality--Juvenile literature.
Classification: LCC GV1469.3 (ebook) | LCC GV1469.3 .H675 2019 (print) | DDC 794.8--dc23
LC record available at https://lccn.loc.gov/2018053423

CONTENTS

PAGE 4   WELCOME TO THE ARCADE

PAGE 6   DATA FILE: WORLD-BUILDING GAMES

PAGE 8   FACT FILE: PLANET COASTER

PAGE 10   TECH TALK

PAGE 12   FACT FILE: THE SIMS

PAGE 14   BUILDING WORLDS

PAGE 16   FACT FILE: MINECRAFT

PAGE 18   GET YOUR GAME ON

PAGE 20   FACT FILE: AVEN COLONY

PAGE 22   CONSOLE PROFILE: MOBILE GAMING

PAGE 24   FACT FILE: STARDEW VALLEY

PAGE 26   PRO TALK

PAGE 28   FACT FILE: LEGO WORLDS

PAGE 30   LEARNING MORE

PAGE 31   GLOSSARY

PAGE 32   INDEX

WELCOME TO THE ARCADE

If you can dream it, you can build it! This guide will help you develop your gaming skills, taking you from building blocks to skyscrapers in the world of **virtual** building. Do you dream of building yourself a giant castle on a hill, or designing a city with everything people will need to survive and thrive? If so, you're in the right place! So what are you waiting for? Let's get your game on!

Hello, gamer! I'm here to show you the ropes. We're in a totally empty world, with nothing but a shovel. How will we stay warm? Where will we live? We need to get building! Follow me...

Before the building begins, let's make sure we know the basics. A video game is an **electronic** game. A player uses a device to create action on a screen. That screen is typically a television or a personal computer (PC), but you can play games on smartphones, handheld gaming devices, or tablets. To play on your television you will need a **console**. There are many different types of video games—from epic action-adventure games and racing games to super-cool **stealth** games which require lots of secret planning and wearing creative disguises. Everyone can find something to love in a video game!

Okay, I think I've got the **foundations** in. What kind of building should this be? Let's go find out!

<<Player One... Ready...?>>

ARCADE

DATA FILE: WORLD-BUILDING GAMES

There are lots of games that let us build things, and they come in different shapes and sizes. Some games will put players in charge of a single building that needs to be expanded with new rooms, while others will let you create a **network** of railway tracks or a theme park full of roller coasters. There are even some games that will let you build whatever you want on a large piece of land or even on an entire planet. World-building games are designed to let players express their creativity. Your imagination really is the limit! So let's use our **resources** and learn all about the games that will let us build to our heart's content.

Okay, Arcade, let's build our knowledge. Load data.

<<LOADING... DATA LEVEL ONE: WHAT ARE WORLD-BUILDING GAMES?>>

BUILDINGS

$ 34,742
60,158

RESOURCES

TOOLS

TYCOON

If you like to build businesses instead of empires, tycoon games will let you build things such as networks of railways or a theme park full of rides.

CITY BUILDERS

Whether you're running a **colony** on Mars or setting up a **medieval** village, there are games that let you build a community and help it to grow and **prosper**.

CRAFTING

Crafting was originally just a **mechanic** that appeared in other games, but eventually people realized that it was often the most fun part of the game.

GOD GAMES

Some games let you play as a creator of worlds, reigning from above and issuing orders to your people on the ground.

BUILDING BLOCKS

Minecraft not only lets you craft, but it also lets you build with what you create. LEGO Worlds is another example of a game that lets your imagination run wild.

SECOND LIVES

Games like The Sims and Second Life let players walk in the shoes of someone else for a short while, living out your dreams in a virtual world.

FACT FILE: PLANET COASTER

Planet Coaster is what you might call a tycoon game, or a game that gives players the chance to run a business and grow it until it is busy with lots of customers. In this case, your business is a theme park, and your customers are the people who come to have fun and ride on the attractions. Other tycoon games let you build and manage railways or zoos.

Planet Coaster is a game inspired by a classic game called Roller Coaster Tycoon. Both games focus on—you guessed it—roller coasters! Have you been to a theme park with your family or friends? If you have, you will know that often the best and most popular rides are the biggest roller coasters. These rides are designed to make you feel excited and maybe even a little bit scared. With their twisting tracks and super speeds, roller coasters make people feel like they're in danger when they're actually not. In games like Planet Coaster, you get to design your own roller coasters and attract people to come and ride them.

It's not all about high-speed thrills, though. Theme parks have all sorts of different attractions. The trick in a game such as Planet Coaster is to get a good balance in your park. You need to provide a nice range of activities for the people who visit, hopefully making them happy in the process.

Building a business and watching it grow might not sound like a lot of fun, but there's something very satisfying about building your own theme park from scratch and creating a place where people can have a lot of fun. So whether you are creating parks or zoos or railway empires, if you like to design and build, then you will definitely enjoy games such as Planet Coaster.

TECH TALK

If you're going to reach for the skies while building and creating, you need to know what you're talking about. This data file will provide the knowledge you need to get started. Okay, Arcade, we're ready to begin.

<<LOADING... DATA LEVEL TWO: WHAT YOU NEED TO KNOW>>

SOLO BUILDING

A lot of building games are single-player experiences. The player is given complete control of the game world, allowing them the time and space to create something truly unique and defined by the player.

SHARED WORLD

Not all building games are solo affairs. Some will let you bring a friend or two along to help with the heavy lifting, or you can save your world and send it to a friend who can explore it in their own time.

VISUALS

Some games let you play in third person, where you view your character and the action from the outside. First person means you play as if looking out of your character's eyes. A top-down view means you watch the action from above.

GET CREATIVE

Designers know that people who like building games often only are interested in letting their creativity run free. This is why a lot of games come with a creative mode that lets you do whatever you want, thanks to unlimited resources and a health bar that never goes down regardless of what you do.

ADVENTUROUS BUILDING

While some people might prefer the freedom to create, others enjoy having more **structure** to their world building. Story **campaigns** can include focused scenes that not only give you specific **objectives** to complete, but also teach you how to use all the features available in the game.

FACT FILE: THE SIMS

Have you ever wanted to be a rock star? What about a vampire? What about having your own family where you get to be in charge and make the rules? That's exactly what you can do in The Sims. This long-running series of games lets you create a character—your Sim—and then lead a second life with them. If you've ever wanted to see what it's like to walk in somebody else's shoes or live in a vampire castle, then this is the game for you!

The Sims™ FreePlay
ELECTRONIC ARTS
Teen

The trick with The Sims is keeping them on their feet long enough to enjoy their lives, and to do this you need to take care of the basics. Just like you, your Sims need to go to the bathroom, they need to sleep, and they need to be kept busy with activities. If you leave your character on their own for too long and **neglect** them, it won't take long before you've got some very unhappy digital friends on your hands.

You can choose what your Sim looks like and what kind of personality they have. They can do almost anything real people can do, such as buy a house, fall in love, have babies, throw parties, get married, and grow old. Your Sim will need a job to pay for their luxury lifestyle, and you get to choose it. Is your Sim a thrill-seeker? Then maybe they should be a police officer. Do they prefer quiet activities such as reading and painting? Maybe they're destined to be an artist. The choice—like just about everything else in this game—is yours.

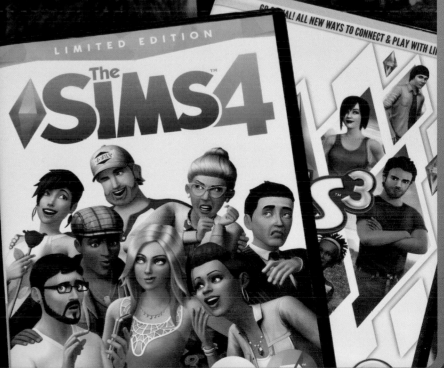

The most recent entry in the series is called The Sims 4, but the studio that makes this series, Maxis, often releases new downloadable content (DLC). This gives you new things to do and fresh ways to play the game. Most of this new content costs money, but sometimes it is free. Always remember to make sure you check with an adult before trying to buy any DLC for a game.

BUILDING WORLDS

When it comes to building worlds, there are always going to be things to make your work more **efficient**, especially if you're playing with limited resources. These tips should help you make the most out of your time on the construction site.

`<<LOADING... DATA LEVEL THREE: ELEMENTS OF WORLD BUILDING>>`

RESOURCES

Many world-building games require you to gather resources from the world around you, whether it be a one-time boost or a regular source of income.

BASE PLACEMENT

Finding the best place to position your base is very important. Resources in the world might be grouped around one area, or perhaps you'll need access to water. More likely, you'll want to position yourself with a good view of the whole area, so maybe look for a location that gives you a good **vantage point**.

MINI MAP

Use your mini map to see where you are in terms of the wider world. Some mini maps let you click on them and move to that area, quickly transporting you to another location.

CRAFTING

When you've found resources, they can often be combined to create different things. Plan for what you need, then focus your searches on the resources required. Learning to use what's around you is crucial.

OBJECTIVES

There are times when you'll be sent on missions as part of a story campaign. These objectives can be marked on the map, but more often you'll have to find a certain resource or build a base or **colony** big enough to support certain types of building.

SETTINGS

You can often tweak the settings to create an experience more to your taste. An example would be the ability to speed up or slow down time. This gives you a chance to take your time as you make big decisions, or to skip ahead quickly to a moment in time when you know something is going to happen or a building will be ready to use.

FACT FILE: MINECRAFT

Unless you've been living under a rock, you know all about Minecraft. But just in case, let's go back to the beginning of this famous game.

Minecraft was created by Markus Persson, but you may know him as Notch. Notch released the first version of Minecraft, called Cave Game, in 2009. This early version did well, so Notch created a studio called Mojang in order to work on the first full version of Minecraft, which was released in 2011. It quickly became a worldwide success. In this game, you can mine the world around you and then craft the things you mine into new materials.

ENDER DRAGON

the End, be prepared for awesome adventure
ous combat. The ender dragon is ferociously
d there's nowhere to hide ...

the End, so you might not spot the dragon
't worry – the fearsome snarls and glowing
alert you to its location. Plus it'll pounce as

TS

×100

15 ♥♥♥– ♥♥♥♥♥♥♥

ve towards you and hit you,
u die.

uch. The ender
fire, water and
s damage from

TIP: Diamond armour will protect you from endermen as well as the dragon, and wearing a pumpkin head stops endermen from attacking if you look at them.

TNT WARNING: Once in the End,
you won't be able to get out
alive unless you manage to
defeat the ender dragon.

One of the reasons that Minecraft has proved so popular is that it offers players a lot of freedom, not just in terms of what you can do in the game, but in how you play it. For example, you can go in Creative mode and start building whatever your heart desires. You can dig down into the ground to hollow out huge underground bases, or even stack countless blocks on top of each other to create towering skyscrapers.

If you prefer to play the game with a bit more danger, you can play in Survival mode, where there are things that go bump in the night. This forces you to build a home to keep you safe. Starting with limited resources, it's up to you to stay alive in a dangerous world.

But wait, there's more! If you've got friends online, you can build together, creating projects that are limited only by your imaginations. Or you can play minigames with your friends and see who's got the skills to score the most points. You can also build your own games in Minecraft, with some of these even going on to become proper games in their own right.

GET YOUR GAME ON

It's still a work in progress, but the walls are coming along nicely. Are you ready to start? Need some more information? Let's load another file. Ready, Arcade?

<<LOADING... DATA LEVEL FOUR: HOW TO PLAY>>

FIND YOUR FEET

Modern games are very clever at teaching us how to play them. Instead of a list of instructions or a complicated manual explaining the buttons, now you might find yourself starting in the middle of the action, and on-screen prompts will teach you the controls at the same time as showing you what you need to do.

FIRST STEPS

Since they are complicated games full of systems that work together, most world-building games will have some sort of **tutorial**. Often the first mission is dedicated to teaching you the basics, so by the time things start getting tough, you know exactly what's going on.

WATCHING THE CLOCK

Time is often an important **factor** when playing these kinds of games. On the one hand, you might be able to speed up or slow down the action so you have time to plan your moves. On the other hand, when you're building things in your world they'll often be linked to timers, and it will take a certain amount of time to construct a new building or unit. The best players know exactly how long each building or unit takes to build, so they can plan their actions as efficiently as possible.

EVERYTHING'S CONNECTED

World building often means many things working together in harmony. You might need to **harvest** minerals in order to construct certain buildings, which in turn need power stations in order to function. If you build too many of one thing, you might find your game becoming unbalanced. Similarly, if you build randomly without a plan, you might not be able to do what you want to.

AVEN COLONY

Some games, such as SimCity and Cities: Skylines, let you build vast cities, while others, such as Anno, take you into both the past and the future to establish your settlement. More recently, we are seeing more and more games inspired by sci-fi movies and dreams of exploring the stars, where players have to try and successfully settle on distant planets. Strategy games, such as Civilization: Beyond Earth, let players set up whole civilizations among distant stars. Aven Colony and, somewhat closer to home, Surviving Mars, have given players the challenge of building a settlement on a harsh and unforgiving distant world.

Players have always been fascinated with the task of carefully and efficiently building **urban** areas, whether in North America or on the next planet in our solar system. Learning the game is a fun part of the experience. You can experiment with different buildings while you try to create a settlement that can support a healthy community. That may mean making sure all the roads link together and that residential and **commercial** zones don't overlap, or it may involve a more stressful challenge, such as knowing that a badly run base could leave a community stranded on a distant rock floating in space!

Most city builders require you to take care of the quality of life of your citizens, but in Aven Colony that extends to keeping the air clear and the buildings secure. If a local storm damages the base, your carefully constructed home could be in danger of failing. The trick is to balance careful construction with smart planning. Only by building a secure and properly balanced settlement will you be able to truly prosper out in the stars. Oh yeah, and watch out for those giant space worms!

KEEP CLEAR

CONSOLE PROFILE: MOBILE GAMING

Mobile gaming has a long history. These days, powerful smartphones are able to deliver **high-definition** (HD) gaming on the go, but it wasn't always this way...

1976: THE MATTEL AUTO RACE

Most people agree that the first handheld electronic game was released back in 1976. The Mattel Electronics Auto Race didn't even have a screen. Instead, it used **LED** lights to tell the player what was going on.

1980: GAME & WATCH

Nintendo has always been at the forefront of mobile gaming, and that started in 1980 with the first Game & Watch. The handheld series enjoyed early success, but it took the arrival of Donkey Kong and the D-pad, which is still in use today, for the series to take off.

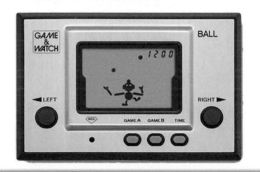

2007: SMARTPHONES

Apple changed things forever with the release of the iPhone in 2007. It launched the era of the smartphone, with tiny touchscreen devices offering console-quality gaming experiences. As technology improves, so, too, does the quality of the games people can play on their smartphones. Tablets are another great way to game on the go, but with the advantage of a bigger screen.

1989: GAME BOY

1989 was a big year for mobile gaming, with the launch of both the Atari Lynx and Nintendo's Game Boy. The Game Boy was one of the most successful handheld consoles ever, with Tetris and Mario doing the business for Nintendo. The following year, things got even busier in the market when Sega released the Game Gear.

1996: TAMAGOTCHI

Tamagotchi first landed in Japan, but the brilliant idea of giving people virtual pets to look after was so popular that they soon made their way around the world.

1998: SNAKE

While Snake was nothing more than a simple game about a snake trying to eat food without chomping on its own tail, it was the first game to bring gaming to the masses via their cell phones, with Nokia pre-installing it on their popular handsets.

2004: DS VS PSP

In 2004, Sony launched the first of its handheld consoles, the PSP. Nintendo released its first DS that same year, and the company has been expanding on the twin-screen concept ever since.

2002: N-GAGE

Nokia tried to go one step further with the N-Gage, a phone that doubled up as a portable console. It didn't catch on in a major way, but gaming on cell phones would undergo a revolution in just a few years' time.

FACT FILE: STARDEW VALLEY

Have you ever wanted to get away from it all, to say goodbye to school and homework, and just get outside and be at one with nature? That's the idea behind Stardew Valley, a game where your character leaves behind their boring day job in the big city to take over a farm, hopefully returning it to its former glory. The game really is as simple as that, at least on the surface, and like other games that have you building and **maintaining** some sort of empire (even one made out of plants), it's very calming to design your world as you like and then look after it.

But there's more to games like Stardew Valley than just harvesting crops. You're leading a second life in this virtual world. Your character must sleep when they're tired, which you will see from their energy bar, but beyond that, the rest is up to you. If you like people, then you can go and socialize. If you prefer some time on your own, you can exist in your own quiet little world, gardening in peace to your heart's content.

You can go fishing, craft new equipment to help you on the farm, grow crops, and make friends with the locals who live nearby. You can go on adventures, such as heading down into the caves to take on some monsters. You can even cook yourself a delicious meal if you like! Stardew Valley not only gives you the chance to live a second life in a charming **pixelated** world, it also lets you escape to the country and grow and expand your world any way you like. It's completely up to you, and that's what makes it so fun.

PRO TALK

Jobs in gaming can range from making video games to writing about them in magazines. Here is some advice and tips on the industry from a professional.

ROSIE BALL

Worked as an artist and writer on Starbound, and is now an artist and designer on Witchbrook, for Chucklefish Games.

1. WHAT MAKES GAMES FUN TO PLAY WITH YOUR FRIENDS?

"I think Starbound is best played with friends because of its exploration and creative elements. You can travel across the universe together in your spaceship, or create a home together! It's fun to all go on the story missions together, too. I love seeing what armor my friends choose, and I'm always really proud of the home we build together."

2. WHAT MAKES A GREAT VIDEO GAME CHARACTER?

"I think a great video game character is one that you can relate to, but which empowers you to be able to live out experiences you can't in real life. Characters that have flaws and insecurities, fears as well as dreams they aim for, these are the kinds of characters that bring you on journeys you never forget."

3. WHAT CAN GAMES DO THAT OTHER MEDIUMS CAN'T?

"I believe that games can teach better than any other **medium**. Because games are **interactive**, they can demonstrate cause and effect very well, and give you a safe space to experiment without any real-life consequences. They can also reward you for correct actions within the rules of the game world, which makes learning very **compelling**."

4. HOW CAN GAMES HELP US BE MORE CREATIVE?

"The fewer options you have, the more creative you become. For example, when I am building a house on The Sims 4, there are only so many styles of sofa to work with. If my goal were to create a **Gothic** house, I need to ask myself whether it could be used here to achieve the effect I want. To me, this a fun challenge; if I always had the perfect items available it wouldn't feel as though I had used my brain very much!"

5. HOW DO YOU BALANCE SIMULATION WITH FUN?

"I think there's fun in simply interacting with a living, breathing world, especially when you have a place in that world, a role to play in the simulation. We are currently making a simulation game at Chucklefish, called Witchbrook, set in a magic school. The surrounding town is full of characters living out their own lives; some of them have jobs, some have family members they spend time with in the evenings, and some are students at the school, going about their studies. You play as a student and can interact with and get to know each of these characters. In Witchbrook, you have the independence to pursue your own studies and interests and decide who you want to be in this magical world, who you want to be friends with, and enjoy living a life you have created. What could be more fun?"

FACT FILE:  LEGO WORLDS

When it comes to building and children's imaginations, LEGO is a name that automatically comes to mind, so it's no surprise this building game transferred so well into a video game. LEGO is loved around the world, and it has been the most popular toy for many, many years. When you think about how much people love to build things both on-screen and in real life, digital LEGO is a great fit.

In LEGO Worlds, you can explore much more than just the world you start on. You can build a spaceship and jet off to different planets too! When players are transported to these various smaller worlds, they can then fill them with interesting creations. When visiting these unique worlds, players can decorate them with all kinds of LEGO buildings and **customize** them using special tools. You can even reshape the ground beneath your feet and change it however you want.

In LEGO Worlds, just like the toy itself, the possibilities are endless. Uncover hidden treasure, customize your character, and race around on a variety of vehicles, including digging helicopters, and dragons! You can edit the world brick-by-brick or paint it in broad strokes, and you can play online in multiplayer mode with your friends too.

Learning More

Ta-da! All done. Nice job, gamer! Are you ready to start a new project, or should we look over the plans one more time?

<<CONTINUE? Y/N>>
HTTPS://STARDEWVALLEY.NET/

<<CONTINUE? Y/N>>
WWW.AVENCOLONY.COM

<<CONTINUE? Y/N>>
WWW.EA.COM/GAMES/LIBRARY/KIDS

<<CONTINUE? Y/N>>
WWW.LEGO.COM/EN-US/THEMES/
WORLDS

<<CONTINUE? Y/N>>
WWW.PLANETCOASTER.COM

Glossary

campaign   A continuing storyline or set of adventures

colony   An area controlled by another place or nation

commercial   Relating to the sale of goods

compelling   Something that deserves interest or attention

console   A computer system that connects video games to a screen

customize   To change something to your preferences or needs

efficient   The best and least wasteful way to do something

electronic   Describes a device or machine powered by electricity

factor   Something that influences an outcome

foundations   The lowest parts of a building that support everything built on top

Gothic   A style of building common in Europe from the 1100s to the 1500s

harvest   The gathering of a crop or resources

high-definition   A high amount of quality in an image on a screen

interactive   Flow of information between computer and user

LED   Short for light-emitting diode, a type of energy-efficient lighting

maintaining   Working to keep something going

mechanic   Rules and methods designed for interacting with a game

medieval   A period in European history, roughly from the 500s to the 1500s

medium   A particular form or system of communication

neglect   To not pay attention to something and cause it harm by not meeting its needs

network   A system of things that are all connected to each other

objective   The main goal or target

pixelated   An electronic image made up of small squares which can be seen

prosper   To improve and become successful

resources   Useful supplies of money, materials, or people

stealth   To remain undetected by cleverly hiding or using disguises

structure   To have a set of rules or plans for something

tutorial   A teaching level in which gamers learn the controls for a game

urban   Belonging to a city

vantage point   A place where it's easier to see your surroundings, usually high up

virtual   Something that seems to exist but was created by a computer

<<SAVING KNOWLEDGE. DO NOT SHUT DOWN.>>

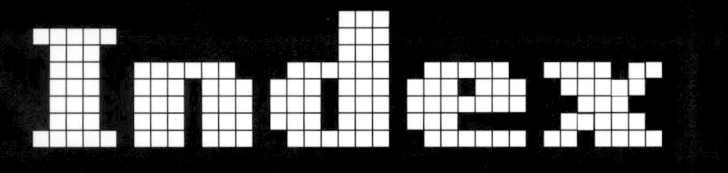Index

A
Anno 20
Aven Colony 20–21

C
campaigns 11, 15
characters 12, 24, 26–27, 29
Cities: Skylines 20
Civilization: Beyond Earth 20
computers 4–5
consoles 5, 22–23
construction 14, 19, 21
craft 7, 16, 25
creative 11, 16, 26–27
creators 7

D
design 5–6, 8–9, 24, 26
devices 5, 22
DLC 13
Donkey Kong 22

H
handheld 22–23
HD 22

L
LEGO Worlds 7, 28–30

M
maps 15
Mario 23
Mattel Electronics Auto Race 22
Minecraft 7, 16–17, 30
minigames 17
missions 15, 18, 26
mobile gaming 22–23
modes 11, 16–17

O
objectives 11, 15

P
PC 5
phones 5, 22–23
Planet Coaster 8–9
players 5–8, 10–11, 16–17,
19–20, 22, 28–29

R
resources 4, 6, 11, 14–15, 17
Roller Coaster Tycoon 8

S
scenarios 11
Second Life 7, 12, 24–25
Sega 23
SimCity 20
Sims 7, 12–13, 27
skills 4, 17
Snake 23
Starbound 26
Stardew Valley 24–25
story 11, 15, 26
structure 11
Surviving Mars 20

T
tablets 5, 22
Tamagotchi 23
televisions 5
Tetris 23
tutorial 18
tycoon 7–8

V
video games 5, 26, 28
virtual 5, 7, 24

W
Witchbrook 26–27

<<THANKS FOR ACCESSING THE ARCADE TODAY. WE HOPE
YOU HAD A PLEASANT TIME. SHUTTING DOWN IN 3... 2... 1...>>